# One Hundred Modern Sijo Poems from Korea: An Anthology

## 한국 현대 단시조 100

Compiled by Min Byungdo
Translated by Jang Gyung-ryul

민병도 엮음
장경렬 옮김

들풀

# One Hundred Modern *Sijo* Poems from Korea: An Anthology

한국 현대 단시조 100

**Compiled by Min Byungdo | Translated by Jang Gyung-ryul**
민병도 엮음 | 장경렬 옮김

ⓒ2021 Deulpul, all right reserved

This volume prepared and published by
Deulpul Publishing Co.
Sunbawigil 53, Gumchon-myon, Cheong-gun
North Gyeongsang Peovince 38364, Korea
(82)54-371-3544
E-mail : mbdo@daum.net, mbdo@korea.com

Funded by
Cheongdo-gun District Office of
North Gyeongsang Peovince, Korea

Prited by Chonwoo Wonsaek

ISBN 979-11-971934-3-9  03810

값 20,000원 / $ 17.00

# *One Hundred Modern Sijo Poems from Korea: An Anthology*

## 한국 현대 단시조 100

Compiled by Min Byungdo
Translated by Jang Gyung-ryul

민병도 엮음
장경렬 옮김

들풀

# Foreword

*Sijo* is a traditional Korean poetic form, whose origin can be traced back to the eleventh-century literary works of the Goryo Dynasty of Korea. And it is still written and widely enjoyed by the Korean people as a medium of communicating their poetic spirit and sentiment. Indeed, I believe, *sijo* might well be named as one of the valuable intangible world cultural assets.

It is also my firm belief that *sijo* is also an elegant poetic form that might attract the poem lovers of the world; however, it is true that it is neither known nor enjoyed world-wide unlike other Korea-originated cultural products. That is why the International Society of *Sijo* Poets had launched a project to compile an anthology of modern *sijo* poems written by Korean *sijo* poets and translate them in English.

The current anthology consists of one hundred modern Korean *sijo* poems whose form can be classified as *authentic*. These days, it is true that there are several formal variations of *sijo*; however, the authentic *sijo* form, composed of forty five morae or syllables (or more or less) arranged into three lines or six phrases, is still the one most widely valued and practiced.

I, with the help of the staff of the International Society of *Sijo* Poets, compiled one hundred modern *sijo* poems written in Korean, and requested Professor Emeritus Jang Gyung-ryul of Seoul National University to translate those poems, and he gladly accepted my request.

I sincerely hope that the current anthology will give a chance to introduce *sijo* to the poem lovers all over the world. In closing, I express my deep-felt gratitude to the Chongdo-gun Distric Office of North Gyongsang Province, Korea, which financially supported this project, and to Professor Jang, who gladly accepted my request and helped one of the projects of the International Society of *Sijo* Poets to be realized.

November 15, 2021

Min Byungdo,
President,
International Society of *Sijo* Poets

## Translator's Remark

    I myself have enjoyed *sijo* poems since I was a little child. And I have devoted myself to studying and critically reading *sijo* poems, traditional or modern, for more than thirty years. That was why I gladly accepted the request of the president of the International Society of *Sijo* Poets, Mr. Min Byungdo, to translate one hundred modern Korean *sijo* poems compiled by him.

    While translating those *sijo* poems, I did my best to be faithful to their original sense or meaning as well as their poetic nuance and implication. And I tried hard to make each line (or each line divided into two or three phrases or lines) of the translated *sijo* poems consist of approximately fifteen syllables even in English version as in Korean *sijo*. Even though I knew the syllable count alone would not make a poem a *sijo*, I could not find other way for the English reader to read a *sijo* poem as such.

    Most of all, while undertaking the task of translating *sijo* in English, I recalled my own ideas as well as those of Ezra Pound, with regard to the translation of poems from one language to another, expounded in my article, "*Cathay* Reconsidered: Pound as Inventor of Chines Poetry," *Paideuma: A Journal Devoted to Ezra Pound Scholarship*, 14.2&3 (Fall & Winter, 1985). And I endeavored to prove that what I had argued in that article could be applicable even to the traditional Korean poetic form called *sijo*.

                    Jang Gyung-ryul,
                    Professor Emeritus of English,
                    Seoul National University

# CONTENTS

## *One Hundred Modern Sijo Poems from Korea: An Anthology*

Foreword_Min Byungdo | Translator's Remark_Jang Gyung-ryul

**Foreword** • 04

**Translator's Remark** • 06

PART 01 | **Poems by the *Sijo* Poets Deceased**
작고 시인 편 • 13

Han Yong-un (한용운), On a Sunny Day in Springtime • 14
Choe Nam-sun (최남선), Sitting Alone • 16
Cho Woon (조운), Pomegranate • 18
Ko Du-dong (고두동), Stars Are • 20
Lee Eun-sang (이은상), Like Bamboo Trees • 22
Lee Byeong-gi (이병기), On the Road • 24
Kim Sang-ok (김상옥), The Absence • 26
Lee Ho-woo (이호우), A Flower Blooms • 28
Jang Eung-doo (장응두), The Wall • 30
Lee Young-do (이영도), Happiness • 32
Lee Tae-geuk (이태극), Full Moon of the Korean Thanks-giving Day • 34
Park Jae-sam (박재삼), The Absence • 36
Park Byung-soon (박병순), No Vacancy • 38
Kim Ki-ho (김기호), Sea Gulls • 40
Lee Woo-jong (이우종), A Coin • 42

# 한국 현대 단시조 100

민병도 엮음 | 장경렬 옮김

Lee Woo-chool (이우출), On a Moonlit Night • 44

Jeong Wan-young (정완영), My Hometown Is Not My Hometown • 46

Seo Beol (서벌), Seoul 1 • 48

Park Jae-doo (박재두), Sea Gulls • 50

Kim Sang-hoon (김상훈), The Village of Apricot Flowers • 52

Kim Won-gak (김원각), At the Dawn • 54

Kim Nam-hwan (김남환), Spring Rain • 56

Park Ok-geum (박옥금), A Pagoda • 58

Ryu Je-ha (류제하), An Ancient Ring • 60

Seo Woo-seung (서우승), Bamboo Trees • 62

Jung Jae-ik (정재익), Winter River • 64

Kim Mong-sun (김몽선), Turning Over the Calendar • 66

Park Kwon-sook (박권숙), Charcoal • 68

PART 02 | **Poems by the *Sijo* Poets Active since Their Debuts**
현역 시인 편 • 71

Kim Jehyeon (김제현), Time • 72

Lee Geunbe (이근배), Magnolia • 74

Lee Sangbuem (이상범), Songs of the Southern Province • 76

Kim Gyohan (김교한), A Trace • 78

# Contents

Han Boonsoon (한분순), A Starry Night with Jazz • 80

Park Sigyo (박시교), The Most Beautiful Name in the World • 82

Yoo Jahyo (유자효), On the Distance • 84

Yoo Jaeyoung (유재영), Lily of the Valley • 86

Lee Yugel (이우걸), A Spinning Top • 88

Im Jong-chan (임종찬), Lyreflower • 90

Kim Youngjae (김영재), Ten Days in the Desert • 92

Jo Yeongil (조영일), The Garden of Life • 94

Min Byungdo (민병도), Wild Grasses • 96

Paek Iun (백이운), A Flower • 98

Jo Donghwa (조동화), Baeknokdam • 100

Jung Haesong (정해송), Crickets and the Autumn Moon • 102

Lee Seungeun (이승은), The Innate Sense, Loneliness, Comes to Me • 104

Park Kiseob (박기섭), When Cuckoos Are Wailing • 106

Kim Ilyeon (김일연), The Sky and the Lake • 108

Nam Jinwon (남진원), Autumn Moonlight of Mount Odae • 110

Oh Seungcheol (오승철), Springtime, Again • 112

Lee Junghwan (이정환), Embraced • 114

Moon Moohag (문무학), The Whereabout of My Life • 116

Roh Joongseok (노중석), In the Wilderness • 118

Shin Pilyoung (신필영), On the Pizza • 120

Kim Sohae (김소해), Gizzard Shads • 122

Park Okwe (박옥위), I Just Cannot But Be a Flower • 124

Kwon Hyukmo (권혁모), Gauguin's Women • 126

Jeong Sooja (정수자), Sad Squads • 128

Kim Bokgeun (김복근), Jangbaek Fall • 130

Oh Jongmoon (오종문), The Desert • 132

Kim Yeondong (김연동), A Shooting Star • 134

Goh Jungkook (고정국), A Fine Day • 136

Jeun Yeonhee (전연희), In Autumn • 138

Yang Jumsook (양점숙), Black Coffee • 140

Ha Sunhee (하순희), An Eternal Signal • 142

Kang Moonsin (강문신), Thought 6 • 144

Seo Ilok (서일옥), The Moon at Dawn • 146

Jung Hyunsook (정현숙), Bokcheon Museum • 148

Park Myoungsook (박명숙), Along with • 150

Lee Jongmun (이종문), The Mountain • 152

Jo Myungseon (조명선), My ID Photo • 154

Kang Hyeondeok (강현덕), Paju • 156

Lee Dalgyun (이달균), Old Master's Devotion • 158

Kim Jinhee (김진희), Two Trees Interlocked in One • 160

Kim Kangho (김강호), Fountain Pen 2 • 162

Moon Soonja (문순자), The Diamond Sutra • 164

Lim Sunghwa (임성화), On the Fruit Flies • 166

Choi Younghwo (최영효), Even if this Country Is Not a Country • 168

Kim Yoonsuk (김윤숙), Vacant House • 170

Jeong Gyeonghwa (정경화), On the Root • 172

Park Jihyeon (박지현), The Door • 174

Chung Yongkook (정용국), Rice-Mugwort Cake • 176

Lee Solhee (이솔희), Dandelion • 178

Lee Sookkyeong (이숙경), I Put Off Getting at the Southern Tip of Korean Peninsula • 180

Sun Anyoung (선안영), In the Night When Luminous Stars Shines • 182

Son Younghee (손영희), The Autumn Sunlight • 184

Lee Songhee (이송희), On the Railroad • 186

Lee Seunghyun (이승현), A Momentary Light of Awareness • 188

Kim Mijung (김미정), Spring Rain • 190

Seo Seokjo (서석조), On a December Day • 192

Sim Seokjeong (심석정), Stone Skipped Over the Water • 194

Han Boonock (한분옥), I See Chusa at the Place of Exile • 196

Han Heejung (한희정), A Cotton Rose • 198

Kwon Younghee (권영희), The Texture of Autumn • 200

Lee Seowon (이서원), Empty Shoes • 202

Kim Jinsook (김진숙), Living Together • 204

Choi Jaenam (최재남), A Thought in the Evening • 206

Park Banghee (박방희), Picking Persimmons • 208

Jeong Heekyung (정희경), An Aged Fan • 210

Kim Deoknam (김덕남), Arrowroot Flower • 212

Sung Gukhee (성국희), Waiting for You to Come • 214

Poems by the *Sijo* Poets Deceased · 작고 시인 편

01

# On a Sunny Day in Springtime

*Han Yong-un*

Petals are lightly falling on the Vimalakirti Sutra,
which I am reading with warm sunshine on my
    back.
Do I need to read those words hidden by the
    petals?

Han Yong-un (1879-1944)

1918: Entered into the literary world with the publication of a poem, "The Mind," in the literary magazine, *Yusim* (The Mind).

1926: Published a collection of poems, *The Silence of Love*.

## 춘주春晝

### 한용운

따슨 볕 등에 지고 유마경維摩經을 읽노라니
가볍게 나는 꽃이 글자를 가리운다
구태여 꽃 밑 글자를 읽어 무삼하리오

한용운 韓龍雲 (1879–1944)
1918년 《유심》에 시 「심」을 발표
1926년 시집 『님의 침묵』 발간

# Sitting Alone

*Choe Nam-sun*

Silent rain is murmuring softly
beneath the eaves.

Sitting alone, I miss the one
who is not likely to come.

Now and then, I cast my eyes
on the gate that would not open.

Choe Nam-sun (1890-1957)

1921: Entered into the literary world with the publication of the first modern *sijo*, "Happy Rewards," in the literary magazine, *Gaebyeok* (The Beginning of the World).
1926: Published a collection of *sijo* poems, *One Hundred and Eight Passions*.

# 혼자 앉아서

*최남선*

가만히 오는 비가
낙수 져서 소리하니

오마지 않는 이가
일도 없이 기다려져

열릴 듯 닫힌 문으로
눈이 자주 가더라

**최남선** 崔南善 (1890-1957)
1921년 《개벽》에 첫 현대시조 「기쁜 보람」 발표
1926년 최초의 개인 시조집 『백팔번뇌』 발간

# Pomegranate

*Cho Woon*

With my crude and shapeless face,
and with my thick and full lips,

how can I let you know my love
as beady red as my heart?

Oh, my love, look, look at this,
this breast of mine split open!

Cho Woon (1898-?)

1921: Entered into the literary world with the publication of a *sijo* poem, "When a New Moon Sets Over the Hill," in the literary magazine, *Chosun Mundan* (Literary World of Chosun).

1947: Published a collection of *sijo* poems, *Collected Sijo Poems of Cho Woon*.

# 석류

*조운*

투박한 나의 얼굴
두툴한 나의 입술

알알이 붉은 뜻을
내가 어이 이르리까

보소라 임아 보소라
빠개 젖힌 이 가슴

**조운 曺雲 (1898–?)**
1924년 《조선 문단》에 시조 「초승달이 재 넘을 때」 발표
1947년 『조운시조집』 발간

# Stars Are

*Ko Du-dong*

It is said that stars are all
brothers and sisters of the earth.

But how are they strewn apart
all over the open sky?

Awe-struck, I gaze at the space infinite
in a mountain temple.

Ko Du-dong (1903-1994)

Pen Name: Hwangsan

1924: Entered into the literary world with the publication of a *sijo* poem in *Daily Dong'a Ilbo*.

1963: Published a collection of *sijo* poems, *Collected Sijo Poems of Hwangsan*.

# 별들은

고두동

별들은 지구와 함께
크고 작은 동기라는데

어떻게 저 하늘이 열려
싸락같이 헤쳤을까?

산사서 보는 이 호망浩茫
놀람 황홀뿐이네

**고두동** 高斗東 (1903-1994)
호는 황산皇山
1924년 동아일보에 시조 발표로 등단
1963년 시조집 『황산시조집』 발간

# Like Bamboo Trees

*Lee Eun-sang*

I hear winds blowing through bamboo grove,
and snows falling at night.

While strolling alone, I pause
under the cold moon of Mount Baek-woon*

to recall our vow: Like bamboo trees,
we shall never bend our will.

*Mount Baekwoon is located in Cholla Province, Korea.
 (Translator's Note)

Lee Eun-sang (1903-1982)

Pen Name: Nosan

1923: Entered into the literary world with the publication of a
 *sijo* poem, "Homesickness."
1932: Published a collection of *sijo* poems, *Collected Sijo
 Poems of Nosan*.

# 대

*이은상*

대숲에 바람 부는 소리
한밤에 눈 지는 소리

백운산 찬 달 아래
거닐다 문득 서서

대처럼 굽히지 말자
다짐하던 옛 기억


**이은상 李殷相 (1903-1982)**

1923년 시조 「고향 생각」 발표로 등단
1932년 시조집 『노산시조집』 발간

# On the Road

*Lee Byeong-gi*

Exhausted all day long, I am not able to walk any more.
And yet, I just cannot let my poor feet take some rest.
If I ever fall on the way, I will make my soul get there.

Lee Byeong-gi (1891-1968)

Pen Name: Garam

1925: Entered into the literary world with the publication of a *sijo* poem, "Let's Return to Our Hometown," in the literary magazine, *Tongkwang* (Eastern Light).

1939: Published a collection of *sijo* poems, *Collected Sijo Poems of Garam*.

# 길

*이병기*

종일 피로하여 걸음이 아니 걸린다
그래도 발은 아직 멈출 수 없다
가다가 쓰러져버리면 넋이라도 가리라

**이병기** 李秉岐 (1891-1968)
1927년 《동광》에 「고향으로 돌아갑시다」를 발표
1939년 시조집 『가람시조집』 발간

# The Absence

*Kim Sang-ok*

Door-locks are latched,
and there are no shoes on the stone step.

It is midnight, not daytime,
but there are no neighbors around here.

Only the lush greens are all I feel,
and nothing is stirring.

Kim Sang-ok (1920-2004)

1939: Entered into the literary world with the publication of a *sijo* poem, "Balsam Flowers," recommended by the literary magazine, *Munjang* (Composition).
1947: Published a collection of *sijo* poems, *Reed Pipe*.

# 부재

*김상옥*

문빗장 걸려 있고
섬돌 위엔 신도 없다

대낮은 아닌 밤중
이웃마저 부재하고

초목만 짙고 푸르러
기척 하나 없는 날

김상옥 金相沃 (1920-2004)
1939년 《문장》에 「봉숭아」가 추천되어 등단
1947년 시조집 『초적』 발간

# A Flower Blooms

*Lee Ho-woo*

A flower blooms, petal by petal.
There I see a sky open.

As last, the final petal
trembles to bloom in full glory.

Even wind and sunlight hold their breath,
and I close my dazzled eyes.

Lee Ho-woo (1912-1970)

1940: Entered into the literary world with the publication of a poem, "Moon-lit Night," recommended by the literary magazine, *Munjang* (Composition).
1955: Published a collection of *sijo* poems, *Sijo Poems of Lee Ho-woo*.

# 개화

이호우

꽃이 피네 한 잎 한 잎
한 하늘이 열리고 있네

마침내 남은 한 잎이
마지막 떨고 있는 고비

바람도 햇볕도 숨을 죽이네
나도 아려 눈을 감네

이호우 李鎬雨 (1912-1970)
1940년 《문장》에 「달밤」이 추천되어 등단
1955년 시조집 『이호우 시조집』 발간

# The Wall

*Jang Eung-doo*

Whenever I hold my fist tight,
I feel I can do anything.

Yet, when l roll round toward the wall,
my mind is filled with sorrow.

In my heart, there's a wall to push
whenever I raise myself up.

Jang Eung-doo (1913-1970)

1940: Entered into the literary world with the publication of a poem, "A Record of a Cold Night," recommended by the literary magazine, *Munjang* (Composition).
2006: Posthumously, a collection of *sijo* poems, *A Record of a Cold Night,* was published.

# 벽

장응두

주먹을 쥐고 보면
만사가 다 됨직하고

벽으로 돌아누우면
서러움만 어리운다

나날이 밀고 일어서는
나는 벽을 가졌다

장응두 張應斗 (1913–1970)
1940년 《문장》에 「한야보」가 추천되어 등단
2006년 유고 시조집 『한야보』

# Happiness*

*Lee Young-do*

While my child is reading a book
and I am doing embroidery,

sitting face to face
with a dim, shimmering lamp in between,

darkness
encircles us,
cautious of our gentle affection.

---

*I once translated this poem under the title, "Warmth"; however, I modified my former translation, and changed its title to "Happiness." (Translator's Note)

Lee Young-do (1916-1976)
1946: Entered into the literary world with the publication of a poem, "New Year's Eve," in the first issue of the literary magazine, *Jooksoon* (Bamboo Shoot).
1954: Published a collection of *sijo* poems, *Poems of Green Grass Cloth*.

# 단란

*이영도*

아이는 글을 읽고
나는 수를 놓고

심지 돋우고
이마를 맞대이면

어둠도
고운 애정에
삼가한 듯 둘렸다

**이영도 李永道 (1916-1976)**
1946년 《죽순》 창간호에 시조 「제야」를 발표하면서 문단에 나옴
1954년 시조집 『청저집』 발간

# Full Moon of the Korean Thanksgiving Day

*Lee Tae-geuk*

The moon you have played with
rises full and round even today.

All the chestnuts, jujubes, rice cakes,
we have prepared with love.

Let us share them all in this land
where wild chrysanthemums bloom.

Lee Tae-geuk (1913-2003)

1953: Entered into the literary world with the publication of a *sijo* poem, "Sea Gull," in the poetry journal, *Sijo Yeongu* (*Sijo* Studies).
1970: Published a collection of *sijo* poems, *Flower and Lady*.

# 중추월

*이태극*

당신들 노시던 달
오늘도 둥싯 뜨오

밤 대추 햇송편에
있고 없고 갖춘 정성

들국화 피는 한 강산서
오손도손 나눕시다

---

**이태극** 李泰極 (1913–2003)
1953년 《시조 연구》에 「갈매기」를 발표하면서 문단에 나옴
1970년 시조집 『꽃과 여인』 발간

# The Absence

*Park Jae-sam*

While all gone out,
a magnolia tree blossoms in the garden,

with half of its branches trailing in this world,
and half in the other.

Ah, the blossoms that fill the space
wherever there's no man around!

Park Jae-sam (1933-1997)

1955: Entered into the literary world with the publication of a poem, "Silence," in the literary magazine, *Hyundae Moonhak* (Contemporary Literature).
1985: Published a collection of *sijo* poems, *My Love Is*.

# 부재

*박재삼*

다 나가고 없는 뜰에
목련화가 피었네

반쯤은 가지를 이승에
나머지는 저승에

골고루 사람이 없는데 따라
고이 여는 꽃이여!

**박재삼** 朴在森 (1933-1997)
1955년 《현대문학》에 자유시 「정적」으로 등단
1985년 시조집 『내 사랑은』 출간

# No Vacancy

*Park Byung-soon*

Full of cars and people, no vacancy is left in Seoul.
In this bustling city, even one's mind is over-crowded.
How can I step aside from this street only full of greed?

Park Byung-soon (1917-2008)

1956: Entered into the literary world with the publication of a collection of *sijo* poems, *A Notebook on the Fallen Ears Gleaned*.
1971: Published a collection of *sijo* poems, *Like Star Lights*.

# 만원

*박병순*

서울은 만원이다 차도 만원 사람도 만원,
맘속도 만원 찰대로 찬 북적대는 서울 장안,
욕심만 가득 찬 이 거리를 어찌 비껴가오리까

**박병순** 朴炳淳 (19*7-2008)
1956년 시조집 『낙수첩(落穗帖)』 발간으로 문단에 나옴
1971년 시조집 『별빛처럼』 발간

# Sea Gulls

*Kim Ki-ho*

Life is but a beehive,
cold as the last day of December.

Yet, the Diamond Sutra tells me
thousand years are just a moment.

Today, with sea gulls,
my mind flies far and free over the sea.

Kim Ki-ho (1912-1978)

1957: Entered into the literary world with a poem awarded at the New Year's Literary Contest administered by *Daily Dong'a Ilbo*.

1965: Published a collection of *sijo* poems, *Wind Orchid*.

# 갈매기

*김기호*

인생은 사철 섣달그믐
생애는 벌집만 같데

금강金剛을 대좌對坐하면
천년도 수유須臾여라

오늘은 훨훨 수천水天 아득히
나도 따라 갈매길세

김기호 金琪鎬 (1912–1978)
1957년 동아일보 신춘문예 당선
1965년 시조집 『풍란』 출간

# A Coin

*Lee Woo-jong*

Like a coin spinning on its edge,
the world is turning and turning.

As I am turning and turning
beside a coin called the world,

I feel choked up by the neck
with those years winding me round.

Lee Woo-jong (1925-1999)

1961: Entered into the literary world with a poem awarded at the New Year's Literary Contest administered by *Daily Dong'a Ilbo*.

1972: Published a collection of *sijo* poems, *Voice of My Mother Country*.

# 동전

이우종

세상은 핑그르르
동전으로 돌아가고

그 동전 둘레에서
나도 따라 돌다 보면

겹겹이 세월이 감겨
목을 죄고 있구나


이우종 李祐鍾 (1925-1999)
1961년 동아일보 신춘문예 당선
1972년 시조집 『모국의 소리』 발간

# On a Moonlit Night

*Lee Woo-chool*

On a moonlit night as awesomely bright as a
 sunny day,
buckwheat flowers adorn the hill white with their
 dewy petals,
while insects gone asleep at the lullaby of barking
 dogs.

Lee Woo-chool (1923-1985)

1961: Entered into the literary world with a poem awarded at the New Year's Literary Contest administered by *Daily Chosun Ilbo*.
1970: Published a collection of *sijo* poems, *Bell Tower*.

# 달밤

*이우출*

달이 째지도록 대낮같이 밝은 밤에
메밀꽃 하얀 언덕 이슬 고운 꽃 이파리
머언 데 개 짖는 소리에 풀벌레는 잠이 들고


이우출 李禹出 (1923-1985)

1961년 조선일보 신춘문예 당선
1970년 시조집 『종루』 발간

# My Hometown Is Not My Hometown

*Jeong Wan-young*

When I had gone to my hometown, I could not
 find it anywhere.
When I had returned from my hometown, there I
 could find one.
I came back, only herding the memory of black
 goats bleating.

Jeong Wan-young (1919-2016)

1962: Entered into the literary world with a poem awarded at the New Year's Literary Contest administered by *Daily Chosun Ilbo*.

1969: Published a collection of *sijo* poems, *A Record of the Collected Vernal Spirits*.

# 고향보다 더 먼 고향

*정완영*

고향을 찾아가니 고향은 거기 없고
고향에서 돌아오니 고향은 거기 있고
흑염소 울음소리만 내가 몰고 왔네요

**정완영** 鄭椀永 (1919-2016)
1962년 조선일보 신춘문예 당선
1969년 시조집 『채춘보(採春譜)』 발간

# Seoul 1

*Seo Beol*

Today, I came to Seoul
only to buy tons of solitude.

How I wish to sprinkle it all over,
like mist, like drizzle!

In my empty pocket is
just a name card of my old friend.

Seo Beol (1939-2005)
1961: Entered into the literary world with the publication of a collection of *sijo* poems, *Sky-Blue Colored Sunday*.
1971: Published a collection of *sijo* poems, *Poems of Square Wood Bars*.

# 서울 · 1

*서벌*

내 오늘 서울에 와
만평 적막을 사다

안개처럼 가랑비처럼
흩고 막 뿌릴까 보다

바닥난 호주머니엔
주고 간 벗의 명함

서벌 徐伐 (1939-2005)

1961년 시조집 『하늘색 일요일』으로 문단에 나옴
1971년 시조집 『각목집(角木集)』 발간

# Sea Gulls

*Park Jae-doo*

Over the western sky, sad and lonely is the
glowing sunset.
Sea gulls are fluttering their aching wings over
the cloud
only to find a place to let their wings take some
rest, ah, in vain.

Park Jae-doo (1936-2004)

1965: Entered into the literary world with a poem awarded at the New Year's Literary Contest administered by *Daily Dong'a Ilbo*.

2004: Published a collection of *sijo* poems, *Some Words on Mugwort Roots*.

# 갈매기

*박재두*

슬프고 외롭기는 서녘 불타는 노을
하늘을 저어 파닥이다 아픈 날개
깃 하나 접을 곳 없어 구름으로 펼친다

**박재두** 朴在斗 (1936-2004)
1965년 동아일보 신춘문예 당선
2004년 시조집 『쑥뿌리 사설』 발간

# The Village of Apricot Flowers

*Kim Sang-hoon*

So lovely are the apricot flowers blossoming in
 the village.
Even the faded ones are as fair as the blossoming
 ones.
Oh, I wish our road to death would be such a
 flowery one!

Kim Sang-hoon (1936-2016)

1967: Entered into the literary world with a poem awarded at the New Year's Literary Contest administered by *Daily Maeil Shinmoon*.

1989: Published a collection of *sijo* poems, *Dance of Wooreuk*.

# 행화촌

*김상훈*

살구꽃 피는 마을 피는 꽃이 저리 곱다
피는 꽃 그 너머로 지는 꽃도 어여쁘다
목숨도 오가는 날이 저리 환한 꽃길이고저

**김상훈** 金尙勳 (1936-2016)
1967년 매일신문 신춘문예 당선
1989년 시조집 『우륵의 춤』 발간

# At the Dawn

*Kim Won-gak*

As if a school of sweetfish are swarming in the faraway sea,
as if their silvery scales are noisily scattering in the air,
all the signs of autumn morning has come to shine upon me.

Kim Won-gak (1941-2016)
1972: Entered into the literary world with a poem awarded at the New Year's Literary Contest administered by *Daily Dong'a Ilbo*.
2015: Published a collection of *sijo* poems, *Thoughts of a Snail*.

# 새벽

*김원각*

먼바다 은어 떼들 굽이쳐 가고 있는지
허공에 비늘 튀는 그런 소리 흩어놓고
무수한 가을이 모여 내 몸을 비추고 있다

**김원각** 金圓覺 (1941-2016)
1972년 동아일보 신춘문예 당선
2015년 시조집 『달팽이의 생각』 발간

# Spring Rain

*Kim Nam-hwan*

Your letter continues on and on
without end,

delivering the tidings of spring
with all your heart.

At last, the river once benumbed
has warmed up now to flow.

Kim Nam-hwan

1972: Entered into the literary world, nominated as a New Poet of Our Time by *Hyundae Moonhak* (Contemporary Literature).
1986: Published a collection of *sijo* poems, *Hwangjini and the Moon*.

# 봄비

*김남환*

도무지 끝이 없는
그대의 만리장서

그윽히 봄을 심는
살뜰한 정성이여

마침내 경혈經穴 뚫린 강이
저린 몸을 푸는구나

**김남환** 金南煥
1972년《월간문학》등단
1986년 시조집『황진이와 달』발간

# A Pagoda

*Park Ok-geum*

So touching is the care and love
a sculptor poured on the stones.

Oh, the sutra chanting heard in an old temple
makes me thirsty,

while a cuckoo's song echoing
through the inky vale of sunset.

Park Ok-geum (1928-2005)

1972: Entered into the literary world with the publication of a collection of *sijo* poems, *Pagoda*.
1999: Published a collection of *sijo* poems, *Crossing Over the Mount Gaji*.

# 탑

*박옥금*

돌로 빚은 정이
이토록 사무치나

낡은 고사古寺 뜨락
독경 소리 목이 타고

황혼이 젖은 묵화墨畫에
골을 우는 뻐꾸기

박옥금 朴玉金 (1928-2005)
1972년 시조집 『탑』 발간으로 문단에 나옴
1999년 시조집 『가지산을 넘으며』 발간

# An Ancient Ring

*Ryu Je-ha*

With all the past folded down,
with all the tangled glances untied,

even with the sky of thousand years ago
engraved bit by bit,

it is now rolling away darkness,
making birds come and sing.

Ryu Je-ha (1940-1991)

1973: Entered into the literary world with a poem awarded at the New Year's Literary Contest administered by *Daiy Joong'ang Ilbo*.
2001: Published a collection of *sijo* poems, *Tonal Variation*.

# 반지

*류제하*

긴 세월 접어놓고
엉킨 눈빛 풀어놓고

천년 전 하늘까지
마디마디 새겨 넣고

돌돌돌 어둠을 씻는다
새가 와서 지저귄다

류제하 柳祭夏(1940-1991)
1973년 중앙일보 신춘문예 당선
2001년 시조집 『변조』 발간

# Bamboo Trees

*Seo Woo-seung*

By straining all efforts
to empty themselves even of entrails,

they have earned knots or guts
to make them stand firm even when dead.

Winds are on their side, too,
coming by and going all the while.

Seo Woo-seung (1946-2008)

1973: Entered into the literary world with a poem awarded at the New Year's Literary Contest administered by *Daily Seoul Shinmun*.

2001: Published a collection of *sijo* poems, *A Photography Tour*.

# 대나무

*서우승*

다 비우는 힘으로
내장마저 토하고야

죽어서 큰소리칠
마디들을 받아내다

바람은 저네 편들라
때도 없이 집적여오는데…



서우승 徐愚昇 (1946-2008)
1973년 서울신문 신춘문예 당선
2001년 시조집 『카메라 탐방』 발간

# Winter River

*Jung Jae-ik*

Do not dare to rashly cross
the river covered with thin ice.

Whether you measure or grope about,
you will not know its depth.

If you must cross, don't forget
to hold hand in hand, tie heart to heart.

Jung Jae-ik (1930-2014)

1974: Entered into the literary world with the publication of a collection of *sijo* poems, *Fig*.
1987: Published a collection of *sijo* poems, *Paper Lantern Hung on a Branch*.

# 겨울 강

*정재익*

살얼음 잡혔다고
함부로는 건너지 말라

재어보고 짚어 봐도
깊이 모를 이 강심江心

손잡고 마음 맞잡고
건너야 할 겨울 강


**정재익 鄭載益 (1930-2014)**
1974년 시조집 『무화과』 발간으로 문단에 나옴
1987년 시조집 『가지에 걸린 지등』 발간

# Turning Over the Calendar

*Kim Mong-sun*

Calming down all the winds,
I gather my uneasy breath and sigh.

And, when I lightly turn over
a page of the calender,

I see a new month coming
to, like a whip, force my life to spin.

Kim Mong-sun (1940-2014)

1977: Entered into the literary world, nominated as a New Poet of Our Time by *Wolgan Moonhak* (Monthly Literature).

1996: Published a collection of *sijo* poems, *Getting Used to Be Alone*.

# 달력을 넘기며

*김몽선*

숱한 바람 재우며
힘겹게 몰아쉰 숨

달랑 한 장 종이쪽을
가볍게 넘겨보면

팽이채 아픈 종아리
다시 사는 새달 된다

---

김몽선 金夢船 (1940-2014)
1977년 《월간문학》 등단
1996년 시조집 『쓸쓸해지는 연습』 발간

# Charcoal

*Park Kwon-sook*

There were days and nights when my life was
       forced to be burnt raw.
Now I take all the pains, and keep the embers
       deeper inside me,
for I wish to make you, the pure golden light, all
       the more bright.

Park Kwon-sook (1962-2021)

1991: Entered into the literary world with a poem awarded the first prize at the Joong'ang *Sijo* Contest, administered by *Daily Joong'ang Ilbo*.

2001: Published a collection of *sijo* poems, *Flowers of Time*.

# 숯

*박권숙*

생으로 타는 목숨이 아픈 날도 있었다
이제 내 안에 불을 가두어 견딤은
순금 빛 그대 불빛을 더욱 빛내기 위함이다

**박권숙** 朴權淑 (1962-2021)
1991년 중앙일보 연말 장원 등단
2001년 시조집 『시간의 꽃』 발간

Poems by the *Sijo* Poets Active since Their Debuts · 현역 시인 편

02

# Time

*Kim Jehyeon*

Oh, time, you are always silent,
and you are never visible.

Oh, time, you do not come to me,
nor do you go away.

You just stand there still,
ever filled up, and ever emptied.

Kim Jehyeon

1960: Entered into the literary world with a poem awarded at the New Year's Literary Contest administered by *Daily Chosun Ilbo*.
2016: Published a collection of *sijo* poems, *Dialect*.

# 시간

*김제현*

시간은 말이 없다
보이지도 않는다

시간은 오지도 않고
가지도 않는다

언제나 그 자리에서 그대로
가득 차 있고 텅 비어 있다

김제현
1960년 조선일보 신춘문예로 등단
2016년 시조집 『사루리』 발간

# Magnolia

*Lee Geunbe*

My sister, those burning charcoals of yours
when you were twenty;

those yarns of sorrow of yours
you were weaving every night;

and, my sister, your smile as soft as silk:
all are in bloom like tears!

Lee Geunbe

1961: Entered into the literary world with a poem awarded at the New Year's Literary Contest administered by *Daily Chosun Ilbo* and by *Daily Seoul Shinmoon*.
2006: Published a collection of *sijo* poems, *And the Moon Bites the Sun*.

# 목련

*이근배*

누이야 네 스무 살 적
이글거리던 숯불

밤마다 물레질로
뽑아 올리던 슬픔

누이야 네 명주 빛 웃음이
눈물처럼 피었다

**이근배**
1961년 조선일보, 서울신문 신춘문예 당선
2006년 시조집 『달은 해를 물고』 발간

# Songs of the Southern Province

*Lee Sangbuem*

Who is crossing the mountain pass with songs
    heavy on his back?
Somewhere here must be a pub where I can
    appease my thirsty soul.
Only the howling snowstorm makes my mountain-like grief adrift.

Lee Sangbuem

1965: Entered into the literary world with a poem awarded at the New Year's Literary Contest administered by *Daily Chosun Ilbo*.

2011: Published a collection of *sijo* poems, *Book of Poetry: Grass Flowers*.

# 남도창

*이상범*

소리를 짊어지고 누가 영을 넘는가
이쯤 해 혼을 축일 주막집도 있을 법한데
목이 쉰 눈보라 소리가 산 같은 한을 옮긴다

**이상범**
1965년 조선일보 신춘문예 당선
2011년 시조집 『풀꽃 시경』 발간

# A Trace

*Kim Gyohan*

We must enjoy flower petals
before they wither away.

If you know, life is but a pursuit
of a trace large or small;

and our footsteps coming and going
are nothing but a trice.

Kim Gyohan

1966: Entered into the literary world, recommended by the poetry journal, *Sijo Moonhak* (*Sijo* as a Literary Genre).
2020: Published a collection of *sijo* poems, *A Station in My Sweet Memory*.

# 흔적

*김교한*

기약 없이 지는 꽃잎
피는 동안 보는 거다

알고 보면 크고 작은
흔적 하나 위해 산다

언제나 순간에 지나지 않는
가는 걸음 오는 걸음

김교한
1966년 《시조문학》 추천 완료
2020년 시조집 『그리운 역』 발간

# A Starry Night with Jazz

*Han Boonsoon*

Tender is the darkness,
but it's boring, ah, to the core.

To our thickening chatter
are the stars above humming low.

At our tip of tongue are rhythms moist,
and on our lips kisses glossy.

Han Boonsoon

1970: Entered into the literary world with a poem awarded at the New Year's Literary Contest administered by *Daily Seoul Shinmoon*.
2012: Published a collection of *sijo* poems, *A Love Letter Received on One of Those Days*.

# 재즈 하는 별 밤

*한분순*

어둠은 부드러워
그러나 지루하지

짙어진 조잘거림에
별들은 흥얼대고,

혀끝엔 촉촉한 리듬
입 맞추는 반짝임

**한분순**
1970년 서울신문 신춘문예 당선
2012년 시화집 『언젠가의 연애편지』 발간

# The Most Beautiful Name in the World

*Park Sigyo*

All my life, I have cherished the dearest name in my heart.
Never erased, it hovers over me like wild flowers' scent.

That name,
I am murmuring in tears,
mother, oh, my mother.

Park Sigyo

1970: Entered into the literary world, recommended by the poetry journal, *Hyundae Sihak* (Contemporary Poetic Art).
1980: Published a collection of *sijo* poems, *Winter River*.

# 지상에서 가장 아름다운 이름

*박시교*

그리운 이름 하나 가슴에 묻고 산다
지워도 돋는 아련한 풀꽃 향기 같은

그 이름
눈물을 훔치면서 되뇌인다
어―머―니

박시교
1970년 《현대시학》 추천으로 등단
1980년 시조집 『겨울 강』 발간

# On the Distance

*Yoo Jahyo*

The sun never ever gives up the stars orbiting
 itself;
and it never gives up the little stars orbiting its
 own stars.
Such a distance only makes one endlessly miss
 the other.

Yoo Jahyo

1972: Entered into the literary world, recommended by the poetry journal, *Sijo Moonhak* (*Sijo* as a Literary Genre).
2019: Published a selection of *sijo* poems, *A Winter Landscape*.

# 거리

*유자효*

그를 향해 도는 별을 태양은 버리지 않고
그 별을 향해 도는 작은 별도 버리지 않는
그만한 거리 있어야 끝이 없는 그리움

**유자효**
1972년 《시조문학》 등단
2019년 시선집 『세한도』 발간

# Lily of the Valley

*Yoo Jaeyoung*

Treading alone, I looked back
to the flowers swaying by the road.

And there I saw the silver bells
hidden deep in the valley,

with whose clear ringing
even the mountains were resonating.

Yoo Jaeyoung

1973: Entered into the literary world, recommended by the poet Park Mok-wol & Lee Tae-geuk.
2001: Published a collection of *sijo* poems, *The Hour of Sunshine*.

## 은방울꽃

유재영


뒤돌아본 길에는
흔들리는 꽃이 있다

골짝 깊이 숨겨 둔
새하얀 은종처럼

댕 댕 댕 우는 소리에
산도 울컥 하는 꽃




**유재영**
1973년 시 박목월, 시조 이태극 추천으로 문단에 나옴.
2001년 시조집 『햇빛 시간』 발간

# A Spinning Top

*Lee Yugel*

Whip the side of my body hard until you would
    see a rainbow.
Spinning upright, I will attest to the agony you'd
    gone through.
Oh, look, the hollyhock blooming all over on pain
    of being whipped.

Lee Yugel

1973: Entered into the literary world, recommended by the poetry journal, *Hyundae Sihak* (Contemporary Poetic Art).
2013: Published a collection of *sijo* poems, *Resident Card*.

# 팽이

*이우걸*

쳐라, 가혹한 매여 무지개가 보일 때까지
나는 꼿꼿이 서서 너를 증언하리라
무수한 고통을 건너 피어나는 접시꽃 하나.

**이우걸**
1973년 《현대시학》 추천 등단
2013년 시조집 『주민등록증』 발간

# Lyreflower

*Im Jong-chan*

Oh, how I wish to cherish all your images in that pouch-like flower!
When the flower is filled with your images, I'll let it ripen into a seed.
Then I'll sow it with love to see you bloom as lyreflower next spring.

Im Jong-chan

1973: Entered into the literary world, recommended by the poetry journal, *Hyundae Sihak* (Contemporary Poetic Art).

1974: Published a collection of *sijo* poems, *Songs of Green Mountains*.

# 금낭화

*임종찬*

금낭화꽃 주머니 그대 얼굴 담으련다
한가득 담기거든 씨로 익혀 묻을란다
내 봄에 그대 얼굴이 금낭화로 필 거야

**임종찬**
1973년 《현대시학》 추천
1974년 시조집 『청산곡』 발간

# Ten Days in the Desert

*Kim Youngjae*

I went there to empty myself, but came back with
 more to keep.
There I was to ride a camel, but was just ridden
 by it.
I went there to erase my footsteps, but, ah, left so
 many.

Kim Youngjae

1974: Entered into the literary world, recommended by the poetry journal, *Hyundae Sihak* (Contemporary Poetic Art).

2019: Published a collection of *sijo* poems, *Night When Magnolia Flowers Are Budding*.

# 사막 열흘

*김영재*

버리고 온다는 게 더 가지고 돌아왔다
낙타를 탄다는 게 낙타에게 끌려다녔다
발자국 지운다는 게 무수히 남겨놓았다

**김영재**
1974년《현대시학》등단
2019년 시조집 『목련꽃 벙그는 밤』 발간

# The Garden of Life

*Jo Yeongil*

The woods are lovely, and it is lovelier as it rains.
O that I were in the garden of life, where I enjoy the rain
and live a life as a modest stele inscribed with a poem!

Jo Yeongil

1975: Entered into the literary world, nominated as a Young Port of Our Time by the literary magazine, *Wolgan Mookhak* (Monthly Literature), and recommended by the poetry journal, *Sijo Moonhak* (*Sijo* as a Literary Genre).
2020: Published a collection of *sijo* poems, *Snow Mountain*.

# 생명의 정원

## 조영일

숲이 아름답고 비가 내려서 좋다
생명의 정원에 옮겨 같이 비 맞으며
알맞은 크기로 세운 시비詩碑로 살고 싶다

**조영일**
1975년 《월간문학》 신인상 및 《시조문학》 추천
2020년 시조집 『설산』 발간

# Wild Grasses

*Min Byungdo*

Day after day, they are cut or trampled,
bleeding and knocked down.

And yet, why do they embrace those sickles
with their own scent?

Oh, I know now why this land is their own
for such a long time.

Min Byungdo

1976: Entered into the literary world with a poem awarded at the New Year's Literary Contest administered by *Daily Han'gook Ilbo*.
2011: Published a collection of *sijo* poems, *Wild Grasses*

# 들풀

*민병도*

허구한 날 베이고 밟혀
피 흘리며 쓰러져 놓고

어쩌자고 저를 벤 낫을
향기로 감싸는지

알겠네 왜 그토록 오래
이 땅의 주인인지

**민병도**
1976년 한국일보 신춘문예로 등단.
2011년 시조집 『들풀』 발간

# A Flower

*Paek Iun*

When you are born to this world, you are already
    a flower.
Do not be afraid not to be a lovely blooming
    flower.
Look, the world is by now serenely leaning on
    your shoulder!

Paek Iun

1977: Entered into the literary world, recommended by the poetry journal, *Simoonhak* (Poetic Art).
2019: Published a collection of *sijo* poems, *Maybe, Poets Are Living Even on the Moon.*

# 꽃 한 송이

*백이운*

그대 이미 세계의 한 송이 꽃이거늘
피어나지 못할까 두려워하지 마시라
세상이 그대 어깨에 고요히 기대 있음을.

백이운
1977년 《시문학》 추천완료 등단
2019년 시조집 『달에도 시인이 살겠지』 발간

# Baeknokdam*

## *Jo Donghwa*

This is where a pillar of fire cared itself and took its rest.
It had brewed its soil for billion years to let azaleas bloom.
And now it is a cold goblet filled with jade-hued years of past.

*Baeknokdan is the mountain-top lake of Mount Halla in Jeju Province, Korea. (Translator's Note)

Jo Donghwa

1978: Entered into the literary world with a poem awarded at the New Year's Literary Contest administered by *Daily Joong'ang Ilbo*.
1992: Published a collection of *sijo* poems, *The Rock Cliff of the Fallen Flowers*.

# 백록담 白鹿潭

## 조동화

태초의 불기둥을 어루만져 식힌 자리
억만년 흙을 빚어 철쭉마저 피워 놓고
마침내 싸늘히 고인 저 비취빛 세월 한 잔

**조동화**
1978년 중앙일보 신춘문예 당선
1992년 시조집 『낙화암』 발간

# Crickets and the Autumn Moon

*Jung Haesong*

Deep in autumn, while crickets are rubbing their
    flesh and bones,
the moon, rusted by the civilization, has cleaned
    itself.
Ah, the boundless, crystalline soul is emerging in
    my vision!

Jung Haesong

1978: Entered into the literary world, recommended by the poetry journal, *Hyundae Sihak* (Contemporary Poetic Art).
2012: Published a collection of *sijo* poems, *Gaze*.

# 귀뚜라미와 가을달

*정해송*

살 닳도록 닦는다, 뼈 타도록 닦는다
문명에 녹슨 달이 옷을 벗는 깊은 가을
무변의 맑은 영혼이 내 시야에 열려온다

정해송
1978년 《현대시학》 등단
2012년 시조집 『응시』 발간

## The Innate Sense, Loneliness, Comes to Me

*Lee Seungeun*

We have the innate sense that cannot be acquired
 by learning.
Ah, it sometimes drives us excited or endlessly
 restless.
And it makes us feel so old and lonely as to crave
 and pine.

Lee Seungeun

1979: Entered into the literary world, nominated at the Nation-Wide Traditional Poetry Contest, administerd by the Ministry of Culture & Korea Broadcasting System.
2016: Published a collection of *sijo* poems, *Ice Camellia*.

## 첫, 이라는 쓸쓸이 내게도 왔다

이승은

학습 없이 갖게 되는 처음의 감각이란
우리를 달뜨게 하고 한없이 불안케 한다
쓸쓸히 간절해지는 나이를 알게 한다

이승은
1979년 문공부 · KBS 주최 전국민족시대회로 등단
2016년 시조집 『얼음 동백』 발간

# When Cuckoos Are Wailing

*Park Kiseob*

When cuckoos are wailing their inky song,
who will set the stone step?

And who will tidy up the shoes side by side
on the stone step?

Spring has hurriedly gone
even with its own soiled shoes uncleaned.

Park Kiseob

1980: Entered into the literary world with a poem awarded at the New Year's Literary Contest administered by *Daily Han'gook Ilbo*.
2019: Published a collection of *sijo* poems, *Riding on a Donkey of Small Stature*.

## 뻐꾸기 울 때

*박기섭*

뻐꾸기 먹울음에
댓돌은 누가 놓고

댓돌 위에 가지런히
신발은 또 누가 놓나

묻은 흙 털지도 못한 채
가는 봄은 가더라니

**박기섭**

1980년 한국일보 신춘문예 당선
2019년 시조집 『키 작은 나귀 타고』 발간

# The Sky and the Lake

*Kim Ilyeon*

After the sky has washed its face with the deep
    blue of autumn lake,
and the lake has wiped its face with the deep blue
    of autumn sky,
they look at each other, as if they were clear,
    wide, deep mirrors.

Kim Ilyeon

1980: Entered into the literary world, recommended by the
    poetry journal, *Sijo Moonhak* (*Sijo* as a Literary Genre).
2008: Published a collection of *sijo* poems, *The Gifted Singer*.

# 하늘과 호수

*김일연*

하늘은 제 얼굴을 가을 호수에 씻고
호수는 제 얼굴을 가을 하늘에 닦고
서로가 맑고 넓고 깊은 거울을 들여다본다

**김일연**
1980년 《시조문학》 등단
2008년 시조집 『명창』 발간

# Autumn Moonlight of Mount Odae

*Nam Jinwon*

Crickets' silvery weeping is painting the autumn night poetic,
and the hills soaring to the sky are wrapped with deep silence.
Did you awaken the void, the ecstasy, the seal of the infinite?

Nam Jinwon

1980: Entered into the literary world, nominated as a New Poet of Our Time by the literary magazine, *Wolgan Moonhak* (Monthly Literature).
2016: Published a collection of *sijo* poems, *The Smell of No Possession*.

## 오대산의 가을 달빛

*남진원*

가을을 물들이네, 귀뚜리 맑은 시심詩心
하늘로 솟는 봉峰은 적막이 만겹이다
허공을 네가 깨웠나 환희심 저, 무량인無量印

**남진원**
1980년 《월간문학》 등단
2016년 시조집 『무소유의 냄새』 발간

# Springtime, Again

*Oh Seungcheol*

Throughout springtime, I just slovenly let those
 pheasants weep.
And now I'm practicing silence through summer,
 fall, and winter.
Do I have to abide or endure this green-hued
 thirst once more?

Oh Seungcheol

1981: Entered into the literary world with a poem awarded at the New Year's Literary Contest administered by *Daily Dong'a Ilbo*.
2016: Published a collection of *sijo* poems, *Arrow Sign in Okinawa*.

# 다시, 봄

오승철

허랑방탕 봄 한 철 꿩 소리 흘려놓고
여름 가을 겨울을 묵언 수행 중이다
날더러 푸른 이 허길 또 버티란 것이냐

오승철
1981년 동아일보 신춘문예 당선
2019년 시조집 『오키나와의 화살표』 발간

# Embraced

*Lee Junghwan*

Embraced, embraced by you, ah, I am embraced by you, my love!
Balmy is all over my world, as I am embraced by you.
All over the world is balmy, as I embrace you, my love.

Lee Junghwan

1981: Entered into the literary world with a poem awarded at the New Year's Literary Contest administered by *Daily Joong'ang Ilbo*.
2020: Published a collection of *sijo* poems, *Cobra*.

## 에워쌌으니

*이정환*

에워쌌으니 아아 그대 나를 에워쌌으니
향기로워라 온 세상 에워싸고 에워쌌으니
온 누리 향기로워라 나 그대 에워쌌으니

**이정환**

1981년 중앙일보 신춘문예 당선
2020년 시조집 『코브라』 발간

# The Whereabout of My Life

*Moon Moohag*

When I was young, the dining table was adorned with flower vases.
As I am old, it is now teemed with bottles of medication.
Ah, my life is nothing but a move from vases to bottles!

Moon Moohag

1982: Entered into the literary world, nominated as a New Poet of Our Time by *Wolgan Moonhak* (Monthly Literature).
2020: Published a collection of *sijo* poems, *Ga, Na, Da, Ra, Ma, Ba, Sa*.

# 인생의 주소

*문무학*

젊을 적 식탁에는 꽃병이 놓이더니
늙은 날 식탁에는 약병만 줄을 선다.
아! 인생, 고작 꽃병과 약병 그 사이에 있던 것을.

**문무학**

1982년 《월간문학》 등단
2020년 시조집 『가나다라마바사』 발간

# In the Wilderness

*Roh Joongseok*

Cries of wild beasts are now all over
as is the moonlight.

In the wilderness
where no man has ever left his foot print,

even the wind and the deep night are all
in wrestle with their cries.

Roh Joongseok

1983: Entered into the literary world with a poem awarded at the New Year's Literary Contest administered by *Daily Seoul Shinmoon*.

2006: Published a collection of *sijo* poems, *Flying Squirrel*.

# 광야

### 노중석

들짐승 울부짖음이
달빛으로 쏟아진다

사람의 발자국은
찍힌 적 없는 벌판

바람도 아득한 밤도
한데 엉켜 뒹군다


**노중석**
1983년 서울신문 신춘문예 당선
2006년 시조집 『하늘다람쥐』 발간

# On the Pizza

*Shin Pilyoung*

Unlike a dumpling or a songpyon,*
you let your lips wide open.

Let the world be honest like you,
and tell the truth as if joking.

Then, one's tongue cannot be hurt,
just because one knows not its stuffing.

*Songpyon is a half-moon shaped Korean rice cake filled with various stuffing. (Translator's Note)

Shin Pilyoung

1983: Entered into the literary world with a poem awarded at the New Year's Literary Contest administered by *Daily Han'gook Ilbo*.
2017: Published a collection of *sijo* poems, *It's a Bypass Road*.

# 피자에 대하여

*신필영*

만두나 송편처럼
말문 꽉 닫지 않고

진담도 농담인 양
털어놓고 산다면야

속 몰라 혀를 다치는
실수 따윈 없단다

**신필영**
1983년 한국일보 신춘문예 당선
2017년 시조집 『우회도로입니다』 발간

# Gizzard Shads

*Kim Sohae*

I am preparing our dinner table with grilled
    gizzard shads.
In the evening, when you come home with sweats
    on your shirt,
the earthly spoons of ours will bloom with flowers
    of our life.

Kim Sohae

1983: Entered into the literary world, recommended by
    *Hyundae Sijo* (Contemporary *Sijo*).
2020: Published a collection of *sijo* poems, *Blacksmith Who
    Is a Daughter of a Blacksmith*.

# 전어

*김소해*

가을 바다 잘 구워서 저녁상 준비한다
땀 젖은 당신도 돌아오는 저물 무렵
지상의 숟가락 몇 개 그 무게가 꽃이다

**김소해**
1983년 《현대시조》 등단
2020년 시조집 『대장장이 딸』 발간

# I Just Cannot But Be a Flower

*Park Okwe*

On a winter night, white butterflies are coming
    on the wing.
One after another, ah, they are coming to me
    unaware!
To those white butterflies, I just cannot but be a
    flower.

**Park Okwe**

1983: Entered into the literary world, recommended by the poetry journal, *Hyundae Sijo* (Contemporary *Sijo*) and by another poetry journal, *Sijo Moonhak* (*Sijo* as a Literary Genre).
2016: Published a collection of *sijo* poems, *Thoughts on the Fallen Leaves*.

## 꽃이 될밖에

*박옥위*

겨울 밤 하늘에서 흰나비가 날아온다
한 마리 두 마리 아아 가뭇없이 날아오는
나비 떼 새하얀 나비 떼 난 그냥 꽃이 될밖에

**박옥위**
1983년 《현대시조》, 《시조문학》 등단
2016년 시조집 『낙엽 단상』 발간

# Gauguin's Women

*Kwon Hyukmo*

To me, life seems nothing but patterns of a one-piece dress.
All those patterns of my life I once drew in utter anxiety,
painted red, blue, yellow, are gone erased by the surf of life.


Kwon Hyukmo

1984: Entered into the literary world with a poem awarded at the New Year's Literary Contest administered by *Daily Dong'a Ilbo*.
2021: Published a collection of *sijo* poems, *First Snow*.

## 고갱의 여인들

*권혁모*

산다는 게 뭐 별것인가 원피스 무늬 같네
빨강 파랑 노랑으로 애간장을 다 섞으며
내 언제 그렸던 화폭도 파도 와서 지웠다

**권혁모**
1984년 동아일보 신춘문예 당선
2021년 시조집 『첫눈』 발간

# Sad Squads

*Jeong Sooja*

Ah, the claws of those wild geese shrieking
    coarsely through the void!
Those snow flakes that melt into the bowls of
    soup of the homeless!
And those apartment housings that can never be
    dreamt of for life!

Jeong Sooja

1984: Entered into the literary world with a poem awarded the first prize at the Nation-Wide *Sijo* Contest in Memory of King Sejong.
2021: Published a collection of *sijo* poems, *Daily Task Given by the Waves of Life*.

# 슬픈 편대

정수자

허공을 찢으며 우는 기러기 떼 발톱이여
멀건 국물에 뜬 노숙의 눈발이여
한평생 오금이 저릴 저 강변의 아파트여

정수자
1984년 세종숭모제전국시조백일장 장원 등단
2021년 시조집 『파도의 일과』 출간

# Jangbaek Fall*

*Kim Bokgeun*

This is a fall thousands of feet high meandering from Cheonji.**
In my heart, I cherish a whetstone that whets myself smooth.
It is now polishing a bead of jade that would never break.

---

*Jangbaek Fall is located on the China side of Mount Baekdoo, located on the North Korean-Chinese border. (Translator's Note)
**Cheonji is the mountain-top lake of Mount Baekdoo. (Translator's Note)

Kim Bokgeun

1985: Entered into the literary world, recommended by the poetry journal, *Sijo Moonhak* (*Sijo* as a Literary Genre).
2015: Published a collection of *sijo* poems, *Rules of Survival for the Birds*.

# 장백폭포

*김복근*

천지를 돌고 돌아 천 길 벼랑이다
내 안에 나를 가는 숫돌 하나 품고 있어
굴러도 깨어지지 않는 옥구슬을 갈고 있다

김복근
1985년 《시조문학》 추천 완료
2015년 시조집 『새들의 생존 법칙』 발간

# The Desert

*Oh Jongmoon*

Since unknown time, men have gone across the
 desert, riding camels,
while camels have come across the desert with
 men on their back.
And, ever since, the desert has endured the long
 night all alone.

Oh Jongmoon

1986: Entered into the literary world with several poems
 published in the poetic anthology, *Here and Now*.
2017: Published a collection of *sijo* poems, *I Have Returned
 Home*.

# 사막

오종문

사람은 낙타를 타고 사막을 건너갔고
낙타는 사람을 싣고 사막을 건너왔다
사막은 홀로 긴 밤을 견뎌내는 중이다

**오종문**

1986년 사화집 『지금 그리고 여기』를 통해 작품 활동 시작
2017년 시조집 『지상의 한 집에 들다』 발간

# A Shooting Star

*Kim Yeondong*

Look, that ultimate word and brilliant metaphor
     of the moment,
that shining thread of light spun out of the depth
     of darkness!
I see a poem written in a stroke at the end of its
     lonely life.

Kim Yeondong

1987: Entered into the literary world with a poem awarded at the New Year's Literary Contest administered by *Daily Gyung'in Ilbo*.

2021: Published a collection of *sijo* poems, *The Country for Old Men*.

# 운성隕星

*김연동*

저 찰나 궁극의 언어 눈부신 은유를 보라
깊은 어둠 자아올려 뽑아낸 빛 한 가닥
일 획의 절명 시 한 편, 고독의 끝을 보네

**김연동**

1987년 경인일보 신춘문예 당선
2021년 시조집 『노옹의 나라』 발간

# A Fine Day

*Goh Jungkook*

When a fine day sets down,
even the sea looks like some children.

Enjoying a good time somewhere far away,
waves have come home

to strew, ah, the memory
of the sea horizon over my feet.

Goh Jungkook

1988: Entered into the literary world with a poem awarded at the New Year's Literary Contest administered by *Daily Chosun Ilbo*.

2014: Published a collection of *sijo* poems, *On Happiness by a Dandelion*.

# 고운 날

*고정국*

고운 날 저물녘은
바다도 아이 같다

먼 데 뛰어놀다
제 집처럼 찾아온 파도

사르르 내 발등에다
수평선을 부린다.

**고정국**
1988년 조선일보 신춘문예 당선
2014년 시조집 『민들레 행복론』 발간

# In Autumn

*Jeun Yeonhee*

The leaves tinted with the love that comes in autumn will be fair.
The leaves falling with the love that goes in autumn will be clear.
Oh, the blue tint still lingering in my memory of love!

Jeun Yeonhee

1988: Entered into the literary world, recommended by the poetry journal, *Sijo Moonhak* (*Sijo* as a Literary Genre).
2012: Published a collection of *sijo* poems, *Ice Flower*.

# 가을

*전연희*

가을에 이룬 사랑 물든 잎은 고우리
가을에 떠난 사랑 지는 잎은 맑으리
지우다 남은 가슴에 파랗게 어린 물빛

**전연희**

1988년 《시조문학》 천료
2012년 시조집 『얼음꽃』 발간

# Black Coffee

*Yang Jumsook*

My world, turning only around you, is as black as
>coffee.
As I can't let it open, my mind is as black as
>coffee.
Sipping bitter coffee, I ask to myself, oh, what is
>love?

Yang Jumsook

1989: Entered into the literary world with a poem awarded the first prize at the Iksan-Iri Literary Contest.
2006: Published a collection of *sijo* poems, *Shadows of Flowers Know It's Spring*.

# 블랙커피

*양점숙*

온통 너 하나로 도는 캄캄한 세상
잔속엔 전하지 못한 그 맘이 새까맣다
쓰디 쓴 커피를 마신다 사랑은 사랑은 뭘까.

**양점숙**
1989년 이리 · 익산 문예 백일장 장원
2006년 시조집 『꽃 그림자는 봄을 안다』 발간

# An Eternal Signal

*Ha Sunhee*

Since her mind has just returned to the day of creation,
my over ninety year old mom sends an eternal signal
with all the strength vibrating in her blood, "Mom, oh, my mom!"

Ha Sunhee

1989: Entered into the literary world, recommended by the poetry journal, *Sijo Moonhak* (*Sijo* as a Literary Genre).
1998: Published a collection of *sijo* poems, *Waiting for a Star*.

# 불멸의 신호

*하순희*

태초로 돌아가는 아흔 넘은 어머니가
엄마, 엄마-아! 혼신으로 부르는
마지막 핏줄 떨리는 저 불멸의 신호

하순희
1989년 《시조문학》 추천 완료
1998년 시조집 『별 하나를 기다리며』 발간

# Thought 6

*Kang Moonsin*

There's an isle that looks like my sister still submerged in water.
Its rock reminds me of her long breath suppressed under water,
and the seaweeds picked up by her, a sixteen-year-old girl diver.

Kang Moonsin

1990: Entered into the literary world with a poem awarded at the New Year's Literary Contest administered by *Daily Seoul Shinmoon*, and later by *Daily Dong'a Ilbo* (1991).
2007: Published a collection of *sijo* poems, *Please, Call It "Seogwipo."*

생각 6

*강문신*

아직도 잠긴 바다 누이 같은 섬이 있다
열여섯 잦은 물살이 건져올린 생미역이듯
섬 바위 되돌아드는 그때 그 숨비소리

**강문신**
1990년 서울신문, 91년 동아일보 신춘문예 당선
2007년 시조집 『당신은 "서귀포…"라고 부르십시오』 발간

# The Moon at Dawn

*Seo Ilok*

Afraid her over sixty year old son might not
    manage it,
mother is cheering him up above at the gate
    opened ajar,
"My son, straighten yourself out, and never ever
    feel timid!"

Seo Ilok

1990: Entered into the literary world with a poem awarded at the New Year's Literary Contest administered by *Daily Gyongnam Shinmoon*.
2020: Published a collection of *sijo* poems, *High Heels*.

# 새벽달

*서일옥*

예순이 넘은 아들 오늘도 힘들까 봐
하늘 문 빼꼼 열고 응원하는 어머니
꼿꼿이 허리 펴라고 주눅 들지 말라고

**서일옥**
1990년 경남신문 신춘문예 당선
2020년 시조집 『하이힐』 발간

# Bokcheon Museum

## *Jung Hyunsook*

The time capsule of Gaya* that is bound for outer
    space
has its door wide open to welcome some more
    new guests,
just after it has set up the route for another
    planet.

*Gaya was a confederacy of territorial polities that lasted from 42 AD to 562 AD in the south-western part of Korea. (Translator's Note)

Jung Hyunsook

1990: Entered into the literary world, nominated as a New Poet of Our Time by the literary magazine, *Monhak Segye* (Literary World).
2021: Published a collection of *sijo* poems, *At Woopo in the Morning*.

## 복천박물관

*정현숙*

우주로 나아가던 가야의 타임캡슐
또 다른 행성 위에 좌표를 찍어놓고
새 손님 태워 가느라 문을 활짝 열었다

정현숙

1990년 《문학세계》 등단
2021년 시조집 『아침 우포』 발간

# Along with

*Park Myoungsook*

Like the sea waves swaying along with mackerels
    leaping up;
like the smell of greens fresh along with newly
    cropped barley;
like the sunlight and the winds turning upside
    down all along.

Park Myoungsook
1993: Entered into the literary world with a poem awarded at the New Year's Literary Contest administered by *Daily Joong'ang Ilbo*.
2014: Published a collection of *sijo* poems, *A Mother with a Mother*.

# 동반

박명숙

튀어 오른 고등어, 그 곁의 물살처럼
갓 베어낸 햇보리, 그 곁의 풋내처럼
덩달아 몸을 뒤집는 햇살과 바람처럼

**박명숙**
1993년 중앙일보 신춘문예 시조 당선
2014년 시조집 『어머니와 어머니가』 발간

# The Mountain

*Lee Jongmun*

Just as I love to amiably stroke the back of a bull
 grazing,
I'd love to caress the ridge of the mountain
 ruminating,
the mountain that is, like a bull, ringing its bell
 now and then.

Lee Jongmun

1993: Entered into the literary world with a poem awarded at the New Year's Literary Contest administered by *Daily Gyonghyang Shinmoon*.
2014: Published a collection of *sijo* poems, *I Will Pay for the Buckwheat Jelly We Eat*.

# 산

*이종문*

풀 뜯는 소의 등을 어루만져 보고 싶듯,
어루만져 보고 싶다 되새김질 하는 산을,
때때로 고개를 들다 요령 소리 내는 산을,




**이종문**
1993년 경향신문 신춘문예 당선
2014년 시조집 『묵값은 내가 낼게』 발간

# My ID Photo

## *Jo Myungseon*

Is it enough to show the image of my face? Can I show more?
They force me to be all smile even when I don't feel like smiling.
They want my ID photo to surreptitiously allure the world.

Jo Myungseon

1993: Entered into the literary world, recommended by the literary magazine, *Wolgan Moonhak* (Monthly Literature).

2010: Published a collection of *sijo* poems, *Ash-Colored Fatigue*.

# 증명사진

*조명선*

반만 보면 다 알까 더 보이면 안 될까
결전을 앞뒀는데 무조건 웃으라니
세상을 유혹하듯이 내통하는 증명사진

**조명선**

1993년 《월간문학》 등단
2010년 시조집 『하얀 몸살』 발간

# Paju*

*Kang Hyeondeok*

Here, ah, here is the final stop,
and we all must get off here
at this final stop of pining,
at this starting point of pining,
where we must drag our unwilling feet,
leaving tears, ah, behind.

*Paju is a town in South Korea adjacent to the Cease-Fire Line between South and North Korea. (Translator's Note)

Kang Hyeondeok

1995: Entered into the literary world with a poem awarded at the New Year's Literary Contest administered by *Daily Chosun Ilbo*.
2019: Published a collection of *sijo* poems, *On the Word, First*.

# 파주

*강현덕*

여기, 여기까지다
모두가 내려야 한다
그리움의 종착지
그리움의 출발지
두 발은 되돌아가고
눈물만 남는 곳

**강현덕**
1995년 조선일보 신춘문예 당선
2019년 시조집 『먼저라는 말』 발간

# Old Master's Devotion

*Lee Dalgyun*

The marsh has devoted itself
to drawing blue mountains ever since.

And yet, it has never been satisfied
with what has been done.

Look, sceneries on the old master's canvass
are ever changing!

Lee Dalgyun

1995: Entered into the literary world, nominated as a New Poet of Our Time by the poetry journal *Sijo Sihak* (Poetics of *Sijo*).
2016: Published a collection of *sijo* poems, *An Aged Lion*.

## 정진精進

*이달균*

늪은 태초부터
청산을 그려왔다

하지만 단 한 번도
같은 풍경은 없었다

나날이 새로워지는
노화가老畫家의 캔버스


이달균
1995년 《시조시학》 등단
2016년 시조집 『늙은 사자』 발간

# Two Trees Interlocked in One

## *Kim Jinhee*

As the pinky flowery winds of spring are locking
   the time up,
and letting all loose the cuckoos' song, "I love
   you, I love you,"
an aged couple, standing on the rock, are adjust-
   ing their dress.

Kim Jinhee

1997: Entered into the literary world with a poem awarded at the New Year's Literary Contest administered by *Daily Gyongnam Shinmoon*, and recommended by the poetry journal, *Sijo Moonhak* (*Sijo* as a Literary Genre).
2013: Published a collection of *sijo* poems, *A Seal in My Mind*.

# 연리목

*김진희*

연분홍 바람소리 시간을 멈춰놓고
사랑한다 사랑한다 뻐꾹새 풀어놓고
산그늘 앞섶 여미는 낙화암 위 노부부

김진희
1997년 경남신문 신춘문예 당선, 《시조문학》 추천 완료
2013년 시조집 『내 마음의 낙관』 발간

## Fountain Pen 2

*Kim Kangho*

Passing the forest of agony, I've finally got to the snowfield.
I am riding a horse that lets its mane flutter to the wind.
Oh that I would not lose my heart, and be balmier than death.

Kim Kangho

1999: Entered into the literary world with a poem awarded at the New Year's Literary Contest administered by *Daily Dong'a Ilbo*.
2014: Published a collection of *sijo* poems, *A Letter from the Port of Paengmok*.

# 만년필 2

*김강호*

고뇌의 숲을 지나 마침내 다다른 설원
말갈기를 세우고 거침없이 달린다
한평생 꺾이지 않기를, 죽음보다 향기롭기를…




김강호
1999년 동아일보 신춘문예 당선
2014년 시조집 『팽목항 편지』 발간

# The Diamond Sutra

*Moon Soonja*

Tell me, is it because
the Buddha's Birthday is near at hand?

In my eyes, even bean sprouts in the pot
look all like boy monks.

In my ears, water drops sound
like words of the Diamond Sutra.

Moon Soonja

1999: Entered into the literary world with a poem awarded at the New Year's Literary Contest administered by *Daily Nongmin Shinmoon*.
2020: Published a collection of *sijo* poems, *It Will Be Clear Now and Then*.

# 금강경

*문순자*

사월 초파일이
코앞이라 그런가

시루 속 콩나물이
까까머리 동자승 같다

톡 치면 금강경 한 구절
묻어나는 물방울

문순자

1999년 농민신문 신춘문예 당선
2020년 시조집 『어쩌다 맑음』 발간

# On the Fruit Flies

*Lim Sunghwa*

Since when, have you begun your careless life
 living on free meals?
How dare you live here without deposit, without
 paying the rent?
Yet, what shall I do with you? Maybe I was once
 just like you.

Lim Sunghwa

1999: Entered into the literary world with a poem awarded at the New Year's Literary Contest administered by *Daily Maeil Shinmoon*.
2014: Published a collection of *sijo* poems, *Winter Salt Field*.

## 날파리에 대하여

*임성화*

무전취식 얹혀 지낸 시작도 알 수 없다
보증금 없다 쳐도 월세까지 내질 않고
어쩌랴 나도 한 때는 너였는지 몰라라

임성화
1999년 매일신문 신춘문예 당선
2014년 시조집 『겨울 염전』 발간

# Even if this Country Is Not a Country

*Choi Younghwo*

Our king is not worthy of his title;
and his subjects are all shams.

No father deserves his title;
and no child thinks much of him.

Yet, even if our world is a mess,
we must clean it to live in it.

Choi Younghwo

2000: Entered into the literary world with a poem awarded at the New Year's Literary Contest administered by *Daily Gyongnam Shinmoon*.
2020: Published a collection of *sijo* poems, *Nondescript Things*.

# 나라가 나라 아니나

*최영효*

임금이 임금 아니니
신하가 신하 아니지

애비가 애비 같잖아
자식이 자식일까만

세상이 세상 아니라도
이 세상 바꿔 살아야지


**최영효**
2000년 경남신문 신춘문예 당선
2020년 시조집 『아무것도 아닌 것들』 발간

## Vacant House

*Kim Yoonsuk*

Ivies have covered the roof-top through winter,
    spring, and mid-summer,
with their hands creeping even onto the stone
    step and into the room.
The vacant house is now stirring with green blood
    flowing on its wounds.

Kim Yoonsuk

2000: Entered into the literary world, recommended by the poetry journal, *Yollin Sihak* (Open Poetics).
2018: Published a collection of *sijo* poems, *Somewhere near a Spindle Tree*.

# 빈집

*김윤숙*

겨울 봄 지나 한여름 지붕 위 담쟁이가
댓돌마루며 안방까지 손을 뻗어 나갔다
상처에 푸른 피 돌아, 웅성거리는 함석집

김윤숙
2000년 《열린시학》 등단
2018년 시조집 『참빗살나무 근처』 발간

# On the Root

*Jeong Gyeonghwa*

Seeds sprouting together won't grow into one and the same flowers.
Plants shedding leaves together won't grow into one and the same trees.
What matters at all is whether they are of one and the same root.

Jeong Gyeonghwa

2001: Entered into the literary world with a poem awarded at the New Year's Literary Contest administered by *Daily Dong'a Ilbo* and by *Daily Nongmin Shinmoon*.
2020: Published a collection of *sijo* poems, *A Bed Made of White Cedar*.

# 뿌리에 대하여

*정경화*

싹 함께 틔웠다고 같은 꽃이 될 수 없다
잎 함께 떨군다고 같은 나무 될 순 없다
뿌리를 함께 섬겨야 비로소 하나 된다

**정경화**
2001년 동아일보, 농민신문 신춘문예 당선
2020년 시조집 『편백나무 침대』 발간

# The Door

*Park Jihyeon*

I just opened only one door, but it led me to many roads.
I trod many roads, but only one door was open to me.
Looking back, the roads I had trodden all looked unfamiliar.

Park Jihyeon

2001: Entered into the literary world with a poem awarded at the New Year's Literary Contest administered by *Daily Seoul Shinmoon* and by *Daily Busan Ilbo*.
2017: Published a collection of *sijo* poems, *Poetics of Nail*.

# 문

*박지현*

한쪽 문을 열었는데 여러 길이 나왔다
여러 길을 걸었는데 한쪽 문만 열렸다
한참을 걸었던 길도 모른 척 낯 가렸다

**박지현**
2001년 서울신문, 부산일보 신춘문예 시조 당선
2017년 시조집 『못의 시학』 발간

# Rice-Mugwort Cake

*Chung Yongkook*

Just recovered from the measles,
my four year-old child is weak.

He's now spreading out his sleepiness
over the edge of sunny porch.

On his head is a rash;
and a rice-mugwort cake in his gaunt hand.

Chung Yongkook

2001: Entered into the literary world, recommended by the poetry journal, *Sijo Segye* (*Sijo* World).
2020: Published a collection of *sijo* poems, *A Cappella of Dongdoochon*.

# 쑥개떡

*정용국*

홍역 뒤끝 속이 허한
네 살배기 붙들이가

툇마루 볕 가장자리에
졸음을 널고 있다

머리엔 도장 부스럼
야윈 손엔 봄 한 조각


**정용국**
2001년 《시조세계》 등단
2020년 시조집 『동두천 아카펠라』 발간

# Dandelion

*Lee Solhee*

Last night in my dream,
I saw you: you were wounded.

Oh, how I suffered from your image
as yellow as dandelion!

Now it has turned into
so many spores floating in the air.

Lee Solhee

2002: Entered into the literary world with a poem awarded at the New Year's Literary Contest administered by *Daily Gyonghayang Shinmoon*.
2011: Published a collection of *sijo* poems, *At Chyongryongpo in Winter*.

# 민들레

*이솔희*

지난밤 꿈속에서
그대를 봤습니다

상처 난 그대 모습
노랗게 아픔이다가

수많은 홀씨가 되어
그대 하늘 돕니다

이솔희
2002년 경향신문 신춘문예 시조 당선
2011년 시조집 『겨울 청령포』

# I Put Off Getting at the Southern Tip of Korean Peninsula

*Lee Sookkyeong*

Let me turn my back here.
Let me put off going to the end.

Eager to get at the end,
but I gave it up at the last moment.

Well done! Let me live more
before I see the end of beginning.

Lee Sookkyeong

2002: Entered into the literary world with a poem awarded at the New Year's Literary Contest administered by *Daily Maeil Shinmoon*.
2020: Published a collection of *sijo* poems, *Black Woodpecker*.

## 땅끝에서 돌아서다

*이숙경*

이곳에서 돌아서자
그 끝을 미루어 두자

너무나 보고 싶지만
이정표 등지고 왔다

잘했다 시작의 끝은
더 살다가 보기로 하자

**이숙경**

2002년 매일신문 신춘문예 당선
2020년 시조집 『까막딱따구리』 발간

# In the Night When Luminous Stars* Shines

*Sun Anyoung*

They twinkle more dazzlingly when exposed to
    the more sunlight.
A star is laying its feet just on the corner of
    another star,
and I, a star never twinkled once, am lying on bed
    near it.

*Here "luminous stars" are the star-shaped pieces of decoration used to adorn a wall. (Translator's Note)

Sun Anyoung

2003: Entered into the literary world with a poem awarded at the New Year's Literary Contest administered by *Daily Gyonghyang Shinmoon*.
2012: Published a collection of *sijo* poems, *Long-necked Flower Vase*.

## 야광별이 빛나는 밤에

*선안영*

햇볕을 많이 봐야 더 오래 반짝인다
별빛 모서리에 별이 하나 발을 걸치고
한 번도 빛난 적이 없는 별, 내 옆에 네가 있다

**선안영**

2003년 경향신문 신춘문예 당선.
2012년 시조집 『목이 긴 꽃병』 발간

# The Autumn Sunlight

*Son Younghee*

Like old parents, it gets thin over perilla seeds
 and beans.
While empty husks and grains caressing each
 other in sorrow,
like an uninvited guest, it timidly lingers on the
 patio edge.

Son Younghee

2003: Entered into the literary world with a poem awarded at the New Year's Literary Contest administered by *Daily Maeil Shinmoon*, and recommended by the poetry journal, *Yollin Sihak* (Open Poetics).
2009: Published a collection of *sijo* poems, *Fluffy Sofa*.

# 가을볕

## 손영희

들깨 더미에 콩 줄기에 늙은 부모처럼 야위어간다
쭉정이와 알곡이 서로 슬픈 듯 어루만지고
뀌다 논 보릿자루처럼 마루 끝에 소곳하다


**손영희**

2003년 매일신문 신춘문예, 《열린시학》등단
2009년 시조집 『불룩한 의자』 발간

# On the Railroad

*Lee Songhee*

We keep our distance with each other,
as if we had promised.

We fix our eyes, like silvery windows,
dreaming the same place.

The wind is blowing softly;
and yet, our yearnings are rattling.

Lee Songhee

2003: Entered into the literary world with a poem awarded at the New Year's Literary Contest administered by *Daily Chosun Ilbo*.

2020: Published a collection of *sijo* poems, *To Become Someone Else in Face of So Many of You*.

# 철길 위의 시간

*이송희*

우리는 약속처럼
간격을 유지한다

같은 곳을 향하여
꿈꾸는 은빛 창문

적당히 바람이 불고
그리움도 덜컹거려

**이송희**

2003년 조선일보 신춘문예로 등단
2020년 시조집 『수많은 당신들 앞에 또 다른 당신이 되어』 발간

# A Momentary Light of Awareness

*Lee Seunghyun*

Amid the heavy rainstorm and roaring bombastic thunders,
we have to pause our journey to seek a shelter for a while.
Oh, I see this life of mine is just the shelter I have sought.

Lee Seunghyun

2003: Entered into the literary world, recommended by the newly launched literary magazine, *Yusim* (The Mind), as a poetry journal.
2009: Published a collection of *sijo* poems, *Light and Sound, and Then.*

## 무극의 빛

이승현

비바람 천둥소리 휘감는 폭발 속에서
잠시 피했다가 또 걸어야 하는 여정
막간에 쉬었던 자리가 이생일 줄이야

이승현
2003년 《유심》 등단
2009년 시조집 『빛 · 소리, 그리고』 발간

# Spring Rain

*Kim Mijung*

As if afraid I might feel embarrassed as I'm of
    that age,
spring rain taps softly at my door and hurriedly
    runs away,
while no one knows it is sobbing for the unre-
    quited love.

Kim Mijung

2004: Entered into the literary world with a poem awarded at the New Year's Literary Contest administered by *Daily Dong'a Ilbo*.

2016: Published a collection of *sijo* poems, *Raising the Tentacles*.

# 봄비

*김미정*

철이 들면 부끄러움 내 먼저 알까봐서
살짝 두드리다 저만큼 달아난다.
아무도 흐느낌인줄 모르는 그 사이에

김미정
2004년 동아일보 신춘문예 당선
2016년 시조집 『더듬이를 세우다』 발간

# On a December Day

*Seo Seokjo*

After driving away magpies, crows are now
      cawing there.
Early in morning on the mulberry tree, what a
      fuss is this?
While rain dripping, a TV has been thrown away
      in the alley.

Seo Seokjo

2004: Entered into the literary world, nominated as a New Poet of Our Time by the poetry journal, *Sijo Segye* (*Sijo World*).

2020: Published a collection of *sijo* poems, *You Don't Have to Pay for It*.

## 12월

*서석조*

까치 자리 밀어내고 까마귀가 울어댄다
이른 아침 엄나무 위 무슨 변고로 저리
빗방울 듣는 골목에 TV 하나 놓여있다

**서석조**
2004년 《시조세계》 등단
2020년 시조집 『돈 받을 일 아닙니다』 발간

# Stone Skipped Over the Water

*Sim Seokjeong*

It is sometimes a star; and sometimes an eye-
 dazzling smile;
and sometimes a knotted memory we shared and
 then broken;
but now just a shadow scattered on the water
 deep and serene.

Sim Seokjeong

2004: Entered into the literary world, recommended by the poetry journal, *Sijo Moonhak* (*Sijo* as a Literary Genre).
2012: Published a collection of *sijo* poems, *Scents Permeated*.

# 물수제비

*심석정*

때로는 별이다가 눈 시린 웃음이다가
그대와 나 사이에 연줄 끊긴 기억이다가
지금은 그윽한 심연 흩어지는 물그림자

**심석정**
2004년 《시조문학》 등단
2012년 시조집 『향기를 배접하다』 발간

# I See Chusa* at the Place of Exile

*Han Boonock*

There's a scenery unfinished either by a stiff or
    coarse brush.
Even when dark clouds tear asunder and
    thunders roar down,
he goes out with a dried worn-down brush to
    draw what he sees.

*Chusa was a man of letters during the Chosun Dynasty, famous for his brilliant calligraphy. He once lived a life of exile in Jeju Island. (Translator's Note.)

Han Boonock

2004: Entered into the literary world, recommended by the poetry journal, *Sijo Moonhak* (*Sijo* as a Literary Genre), and later in 2006 with a poem awarded at the New Year's Literary Contest administered by *Daily Seoul Shinmoon*.
2018: Published a collection of *sijo* poems, *Promise of a Flower*.

## 적소, 추사秋史를 뵈옵다

한분옥

갈필로도 파필로도 다 못 그린 풍경 있다
먹장구름 살을 찢고 우레가 내리쳐도
먹 마른 독필禿筆을 든 채 문을 열고 나선다

한분옥
2004년 《시조문학》 등단, 2006년 서울신문 신춘문예 당선
2018년 시조집 『꽃의 약속』 발간

# A Cotton Rose

*Han Heejung*

With a wide-brimmed hat on the head,
and with fine wrinkles on the face,

she is asking for directions
in the place foreign to her.

At a whistle stop in the morning,
she stands there, looking for someone.

Han Heejung

2005: Entered into the literary world, recommended by the poetry journal, *Sijo 21* (*Sijo* of the 21st Century).
2009: Published a collection of *sijo* poems, *Good Morning, Foxtails*.

# 부용

*한희정*

챙 넓은 모자 쓰고
잔주름이 더 고운

낯선 여행지의
길을 묻는 그 여자

막 깨인 아침 간이역
누굴 찾아 서 있나

한희정
2005년《시조21》등단
2009년 시조집『굿모닝 강아지풀』발간

# The Texture of Autumn

*Kwon Younghee*

Look, the leaves of an age-old sycamore
looks fair and lovely.

That sycamore tree beside a ginkgo tree,
how luminous it is!

I, worn out from life, stand still
beside them under the sunlight.

Kwon Younghee

2007: Entered into the literary world, recommended by the newly launched literary magazine, *Yusim* (The Mind), as a poetry journal.
2016: Published a collection of *sijo* poems, *Time of Misreading*.

# 가을 무늬

*권영희*

참 곱게 늙은
플라타너스 앞입니다

어쩜 이리 환할까
은행나무 곁입니다

사느라 찌든 나도 가만
햇살 아래 섭니다





권영희
2007년 《유심》 등단
2016년 시조집 『오독의 시간』 발간

# Empty Shoes

*Lee Seowon*

A pair of white rubber shoes is
still there on the stone step.

Rain water collected in them is,
ah, clean and crystal.

Father passed away ten years ago;
yet, I still feel his tidy mind.

Lee Seowon

2008: Entered into the literary world with a poem awarded at the New Year's Literary Contest administered by *Daily Busan Ilbo*.
2017: Published a collection of *sijo* poems, *A Small Window on the Door*.

# 헛신발

*이서원*

댓돌 앞에 세워진
고무신 한 켤레

그 안에 고인 물이
찰방찰방 맑아라

아버지 가신 지 십년
희고 고운 마음 하나


이서원

2008년 부산일보 신춘문예 당선
2017년 시조집 『뙤창』 발간

# Living Together

*Kim Jinsook*

Young sparrows are sitting side by side on the
    electric wire.
Soon a sparrow comes and sits on it, the wire
    sways awhile.
All the sparrows are holding fast together till it is
    lulled.

Kim Jinsook

2008: Entered into the literary world, nominated as a New Poet of Our Time by the poetry journal, *Sijo 21* (*Sijo* of the 21st Century).
2019: Published a collection of *sijo* poems, *Tears Are Not Salty Enough*.

## 함께 산다는 건

*김진숙*

전깃줄 어린 제비들 나란히 앉아 있다
또 한 마리 날아와 잠시 흔들리는 그 순간
모두가 하나가 되어 함께 버텨주고 있다

**김진숙**
2008년 《시조21》 등단
2019년 시조집 『눈물이 참 싱겁다』 발간

# A Thought in the Evening

*Choi Jaenam*

An old couple is treading through the dark lane,
leaning on each other.

As if heavily loaded,
their torsos are tilted to each other's.

Look, how they are desperate
not to lose their boney balance.

Choi Jaenam

2008: Entered into the literary world, nominated as a New Poet of Our Time by the poetry journal, *Sijo 21* (*Sijo* of the 21st Century).

2015: Published a collection of *sijo* poems, *Stubborn Nature of the Wind*.

# 저녁 단상

*최재남*

어스름 골목길을
기대 걷는 노부부

무거운 짐을 부리나
기우는 한 어깨를

한사코 떠받쳐 올리는
저 앙상한 무게중심

**최재남**
2008년 《시조21》 등단
2015년 시조집 『바람의 근성』 발간

# Picking Persimmons

*Park Banghee*

When I pull the whole branch,
even the daytime moon is dragged on.
Soon the branch is cut off,
and I can pick some persimmons.
With its red balls of life lost,
the pale sky darkens in no time.

Park Banghee

2009: Entered into the literary world, recommended by the newly launched literary magazine, *Yusim* (The Mind), as a poetry journal.
2012: Published a collection of *sijo* poems, *A Chair Too Big*.

# 감을 따다

*박방희*

가지째 잡아당기자
흰 낮달이 끌려온다
툭, 힘줄이 끊어지며
공중의 감이 따지고
불알 덴 희멀건 하늘이
금세 어두워진다

**박방희**
2009년 《유심》 등단
2012년 시조집 『너무 큰 의자』 발간

# An Aged Fan

*Jeong Heekyung*

Switched on, it makes noise as if it were raining cats and dogs.
Yes, the noise helps the wetness abate through its whirling sound,
but it runs hot all along, suffering from menopause disorder.

Jeong Heekyung

2010: Entered into the literary world, recommended by the poetry journal, *Seojeong-gwa Hyunsil* (Lyric and the Reality).
2014: Published a collection of *sijo* poems, *Jiseul-ri*.

# 낡은 선풍기

*정희경*

스위치를 넣으면 억수같이 내리는 비
덜덜덜 소리 풀어 눅눅함을 지운다
온종일 열나는 모터 갱년기가 거기 있다

정희경
2010년《서정과현실》등단
2014년 시조집『지슬리』발간

# Arrowroot Flower

*Kim Deoknam*

Here is a lady whose bodily scent is tingling my nose.
I, unable to lift even a finger, am just fidgeting,
dazzled at the violet, giddy beauty that holds my waist up.

Kim Deoknam

2011: Entered into the literary world with a poem awarded at the New Year's Literary Contest administered by *Daily Gookje Shinmoon*.
2016: Published a collection of *sijo* poems, *A Wind Flower at Byunsan*.

## 칡꽃

*김덕남*

살내 폴폴 날리며 코끝 스치는 여자
손 하나 까딱 못해 애태우는 나를 두고
뉘 허리 감아올리나 보랏빛 어질머리

김덕남
2011년 국제신문 신춘문예 당선
2016년 시조집 『변산바람꽃』 발간

# Waiting for You to Come

*Sung Gukhee*

Your coming has made my December days melt
    into springtide:
even the cold railway platform seems immersed
    in the haze;
and ice flowers at my tiptoed feet looks like vernal
    glories.

Sung Gukhee

2011: Entered into the literary world with a poem awarded at the New Year's Literary Contest administered by *Daily Seoul Shinmoon*, and by *Daily Nongmin Shinmoon*.
2020: Published a collection of *sijo* poems, *Flowers Bloom Only When Gone Wild*.

# 마중

*성국희*

당신이 오시기에 12월은 봄입니다
열차가 닿고 있는 플랫폼에 아지랑이
동동동 내 까치발에 얼음꽃, 봄입니다

**성국희**
2011년 서울신문, 농민신문 신춘문예 당선
2020년 시조집 『미쳐야 꽃이 핀다』 발간